10 THINGS YOU SHOULD KNOW ABOUT

SHARKS

By Steve Parker
Illustrated by John Butler

MiLes KeLLy
PUBLISHING

First published in 2002 by
Miles Kelly Publishing Ltd
Bardfield Centre,
Great Bardfield,
Essex, CM7 4SL

2 4 6 8 10 9 7 5 3 1

Editorial Director: Paula Borton
Art Director: Clare Sleven
Project Editor: Belinda Gallagher
Assistant Editors: Nicola Jessop, Nicola Sail
Design: HERRING BONE DESIGN
Artwork Commissioning: Lesley Cartlidge
Indexer: Jane Parker

ISBN 1-84236-118-X

Printed in Hong Kong

www.mileskelly.net
info@mileskelly.net

Contents

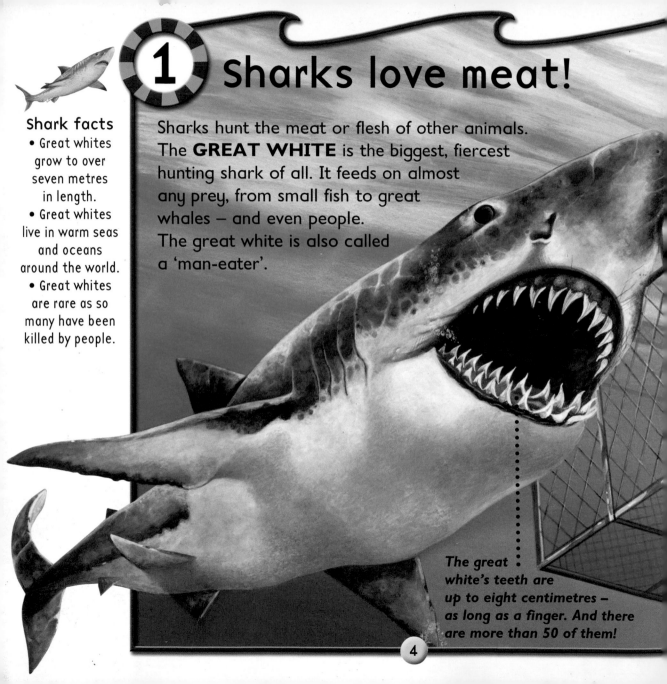

① Sharks love meat!

Shark facts
- Great whites grow to over seven metres in length.
- Great whites live in warm seas and oceans around the world.
- Great whites are rare as so many have been killed by people.

Sharks hunt the meat or flesh of other animals. The **GREAT WHITE** is the biggest, fiercest hunting shark of all. It feeds on almost any prey, from small fish to great whales — and even people. The great white is also called a 'man-eater'.

The great white's teeth are up to eight centimetres — as long as a finger. And there are more than 50 of them!

Great whites are so dangerous, divers who study and photograph them stay in a strong safety-cage.

Jumbo shark!

The biggest great white ever weighed was 4 ¹/₂ tonnes. That's as heavy as a full-grown elephant!

The great white is certainly great, but it's not white — it has a dark grey back, and a pale grey or cream underside, often with dark scars from old wounds.

Sharks cannot chew!

Shark facts
• The whale shark grows to more than 15 metres long.
• Whale sharks can weigh over 20 tonnes.

Most sharks are big. The **WHALE SHARK** is a giant! It is the world's biggest fish, but is not a fierce hunter. It swims with its mouth open, filtering small animals such as fish and krill from the water with its special comb-like gills. Like all sharks, it cannot chew — it just swallows its food whole!

The whale shark has only very small teeth in its huge mouth.

Whale sharks often lie still just under the surface of the water. Are they sunbathing or resting? No one really knows for sure.

The whale shark has a spotty back and pale underside.

Big sharks often have smaller fish, like these pilot fish, swimming with them.

Sharks have super senses!

Shark facts

- The great hammerhead is more than five metres long.
- Sometimes hammerheads have dozens of stingray stings stuck in their throats.

Sharks like the **HAMMERHEAD** are super-sensitive. They can smell blood in the water from five kilometres away. In clear seas they can see for 30 metres ahead of them. They even sense tiny amounts of natural electricity in the water, made by their prey.

Water-wings!

The 'hammer' is like an underwater wing. It helps the shark to swim well and stay up near the surface.

The snout (nose area) detects tiny bursts of electricity in the water which are made by other animals as they move.

The eye and nostril are at the very end of the amazing lobed head.

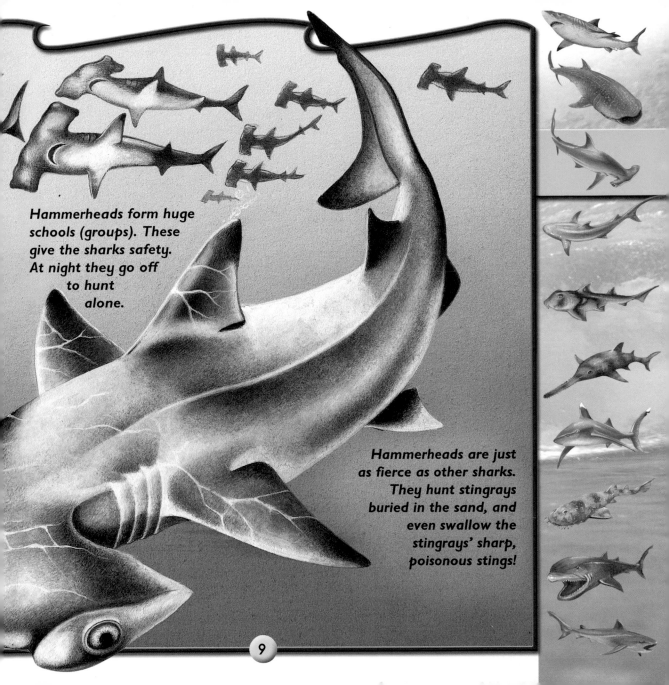

Hammerheads form huge schools (groups). These give the sharks safety. At night they go off to hunt alone.

Hammerheads are just as fierce as other sharks. They hunt stingrays buried in the sand, and even swallow the stingrays' sharp, poisonous stings!

A deadly tail!

Sharks swish their tails to and fro, to swim fast. But the **THRESHER** uses its tail in another way too — as a weapon! It flicks its long tail about like an underwater whip, bashing small fish to wound or stun them. Then the thresher snaps them up in its mouth.

Shark facts
• The thresher's tail can be three metres — half the shark's total length.
• Threshers are also called fox sharks or swingle-tails.

The thresher's teeth are small and triangle-shaped, but they're very sharp, just like short knife blades.

Threshers eat small fish like herring, mackerel and pilchard, which live in huge shoals. The sharks swim through the shoal, thrashing their tails. This stuns the fish, allowing the threshers to swim back and eat them.

A baby is born!

A few mother sharks, like the thresher, give birth to babies rather than laying eggs. The baby is 160 centimetres long.

In a shark's tail, the upper part, or lobe, is longer than the lower one. In the thresher's case – it's a lot longer! (In other fish the two lobes are about equal.)

5 Eggs and babies

Shark facts
• Port Jackson sharks grow to two metres long.
• They gather in shallow water on rocky reefs to breed.

Some sharks lay eggs, like the mother **PORT JACKSON SHARK**. She sticks them to rocks or weeds on the seabed. A few weeks later the baby sharks hatch out. They're hardly bigger than your hand. They look just like their parents — and start to hunt straight away!

Each back fin has a sharp, pointed spine just in front of it — to act as protection against other sharks.

The eggs are attached to rocks or pebbles on the seabed.

12

Port Jacksons are in the group called horned or bullhead sharks. They have a horn-like ridge above each eye, and a wide, blunt head. They can lie still on the seabed for hours.

Screwy egg!

Port Jackson eggs are up to 20 centimetres long. A strange screw-shaped ridge holds the eggs among the rocks.

Small, sharp front teeth in the down pointing mouth grab shellfish, crabs, shrimps and worms. Bigger, flat rear teeth crush them.

13

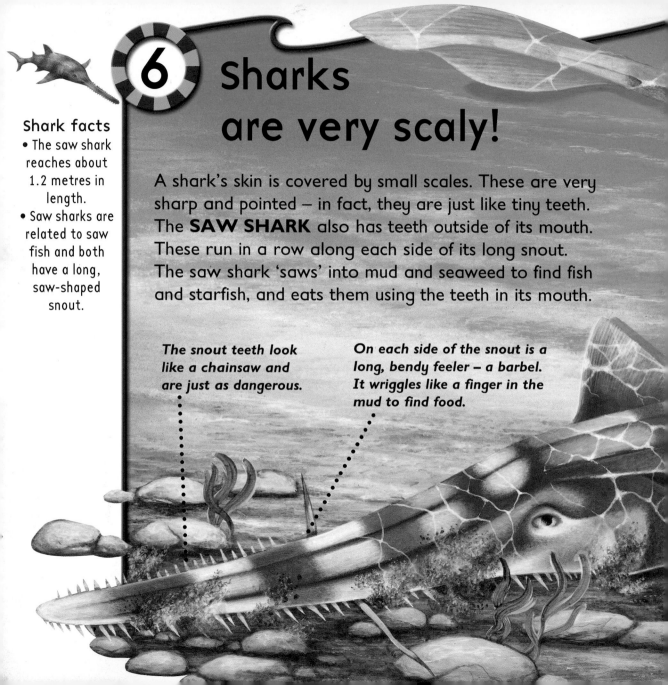

6 Sharks are very scaly!

Shark facts

- The saw shark reaches about 1.2 metres in length.
- Saw sharks are related to saw fish and both have a long, saw-shaped snout.

A shark's skin is covered by small scales. These are very sharp and pointed – in fact, they are just like tiny teeth. The **SAW SHARK** also has teeth outside of its mouth. These run in a row along each side of its long snout. The saw shark 'saws' into mud and seaweed to find fish and starfish, and eats them using the teeth in its mouth.

The snout teeth look like a chainsaw and are just as dangerous.

On each side of the snout is a long, bendy feeler – a barbel. It wriggles like a finger in the mud to find food.

Be a saw shark!

You can make any kind of shark mask, from stiff card. But the saw shark looks one of the fiercest and funniest!

The saw shark has a flattened body which is ideal for lying low! It spends most of its time swimming or resting on the seabed.

15

Sharks like to sleep!

Shark facts
• White-tipped reef sharks are two metres in length.
• They hunt fish, crabs, lobsters and even octopuses.

Sharks don't just swim and hunt. Some like to have a rest. **WHITE-TIPPED REEF SHARKS** sleep by day in caves or under rocks. They often rub their backs against the rocks to get rid of pests. But at night, they go their separate ways and swim off to hunt.

The white-tipped fins make this shark easy to recognize.

These sharks may be still by day, but if a tasty fish comes near – they wake up in a flash!

Close eyes!

When a shark attacks, a special piece of skin called a membrane slides down to protect its eyes.

This big fin, on the side of the body near the front, is a shark's pectoral fin.

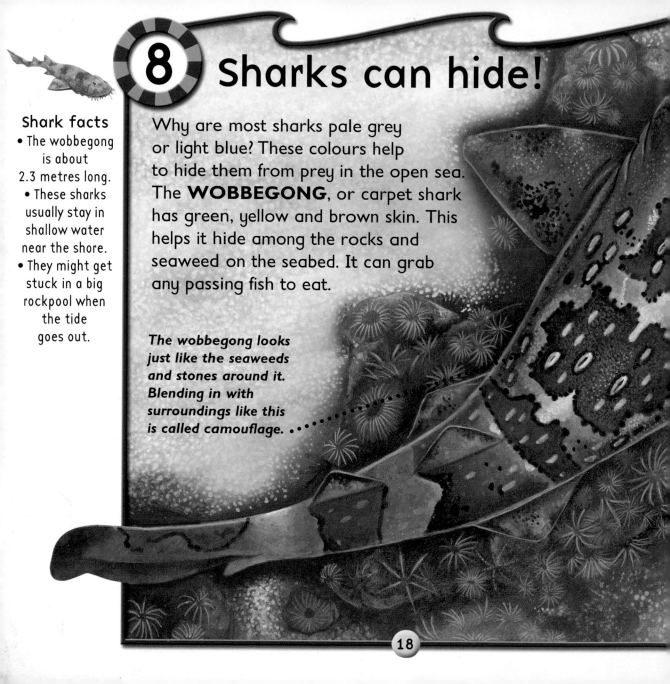

8 Sharks can hide!

Shark facts

- The wobbegong is about 2.3 metres long.
- These sharks usually stay in shallow water near the shore.
- They might get stuck in a big rockpool when the tide goes out.

Why are most sharks pale grey or light blue? These colours help to hide them from prey in the open sea. The **WOBBEGONG**, or carpet shark has green, yellow and brown skin. This helps it hide among the rocks and seaweed on the seabed. It can grab any passing fish to eat.

The wobbegong looks just like the seaweeds and stones around it. Blending in with surroundings like this is called camouflage.

Carpet shark!

Find a carpet with plenty of colours. Get some patches of paper the same colours. Sticky-tape them onto some old clothes and lie on the carpet. Are you well camouflaged, like the wobbegong?

The wobbegong lies very still on the seabed waiting for a meal. It may not move for hours!

A bendy skeleton

Shark facts
- The megamouth is 4.5 metres long.
- It weighs about one tonne.
- Megamouths live in deep water where it is very dark.

The **MEGAMOUTH** is a mysterious shark of the deep ocean. Like other sharks, it has no bones! Every shark has a strong skeleton inside its body, with parts like a skull and ribs. But these parts are not made of bone. They are made of rubbery, bendy material called cartilage.

New discovery!
No one had ever seen a megamouth until 1976, when one was caught near Hawaii in the Pacific Ocean.

The megamouth does not chase after prey, like most other sharks. It swims along slowly.

The megamouth's mouth really is mega! It's about one metre across – and it glows in the dark! But the teeth are tiny.

Like whale sharks and basking sharks, megamouths suck in tiny animals such as krill and baby fish.

The loose skin and floppy fins show that the megamouth is a slow swimmer.

Shark facts

- Tiger sharks reach more than six metres in length.
- They are wide and bulky too, so they can weigh more than 1.5 tonnes.
- Some people who were thought to be eaten by great whites, were probably attacked by tiger sharks.

Some sharks have huge appetites and will eat almost anything. The **TIGER SHARK** eats fish, seals, turtles, dolphins, sea birds, squid, crabs, other sharks, and almost anything else. Tiger sharks have also been known to swim along the coast and attack people in water that's only waist-deep.

In a shark, new teeth are always growing to replace the ones which wear out or snap off. So the tiger shark is always ready to bite!

The tiger shark is big and powerful. It could swallow this monk seal in one gulp.

22

Tiger sharks are born with stripes on their sides. These fade as the shark gets older.

Dustbin shark!

Tiger sharks have swallowed leftover food thrown from ships, also tin cans, lumps of wood, training shoes, and even a tom-tom – a type of drum!

Tiger sharks can be big and heavy. Some can even rival great whites in size.

Index